Zig Misiak: Author   Jennifer Bettio: Illustrator
Educational consultant: Shaylyn Misiak, ECE, BEd, BA (hons.), OCT
Revised 2022, ISBN 978-0-9950128-3-7

Other publications by Zig Misiak

FIRST NATIONS RESOURCE COLLECTION, ISBN 978-0-9811880-2-7
WAMPUM: The Story of Shaylyn the Clam, ISBN-978-0-9811880-8-9
WAR of 1812: Highlighting Native Nations, ISBN 978-0-9811880-5-8
WAR of 1812: Western Hooves of Thunder, ISBN 978-0-9811880-3-4
TONTO: The Man in Front of the Mask, ISBN 978-0-9811880-6-5
4 in 1 LEARNING: French & English, ISBN 978-0-9950128-0-6
ABC's Colouring Book, ISBN 978-0-9950128-9-9
1-2-3's, Shapes & Colours Colouring Book, ISBN 978-1-7771417-0-7
ASHER: of the Heron Clan, ISBN 978-0-9950128-3-7
COLTON: of the Bear Clan, ISBN 978-8-9950128-2-0
CRISTINE: of the Snipe Clan, ISBN 978-0-9950128-7-5
DARYL: of the Deer Clan, ISBN 978-0-9950128-6-8
LUKE: of the Eel Clan, ISBN 978-1-7771417-7-6
MEAGHAN: of the Hawk Clan, ISBN 978-0-9950128-8-2
RYAN: of the Wolf Clan, ISBN 978-0-9950128-5-1
STANLEY: of the Beaver Clan, ISBN 978-1-7771417-8-3
TYLER: of the Turtle Clan, ISBN 978-0-9950128-1-3
POLISH Heritage Guide, ISBN 978-1-7771417-5-2

www.canadianauthoreducation.com

Contents

Dedicated to Sharon Kotow Misiak
December 14, 1953—May 24, 2001
Mother of Ryan, Tyler, Daryl & Shaylyn

I

Her eyes open wide

Exposed at low tide

This shell, natural and wild

Picked up by a child

Carried to a village circle

There broken for her purple

All parts of her were used

Nothing wasted nor abused

Like a caterpillar to a butterfly

Changing under the blue sky

Not the same but a different glory

Into the word, into the story

By: Zig Misiak

II

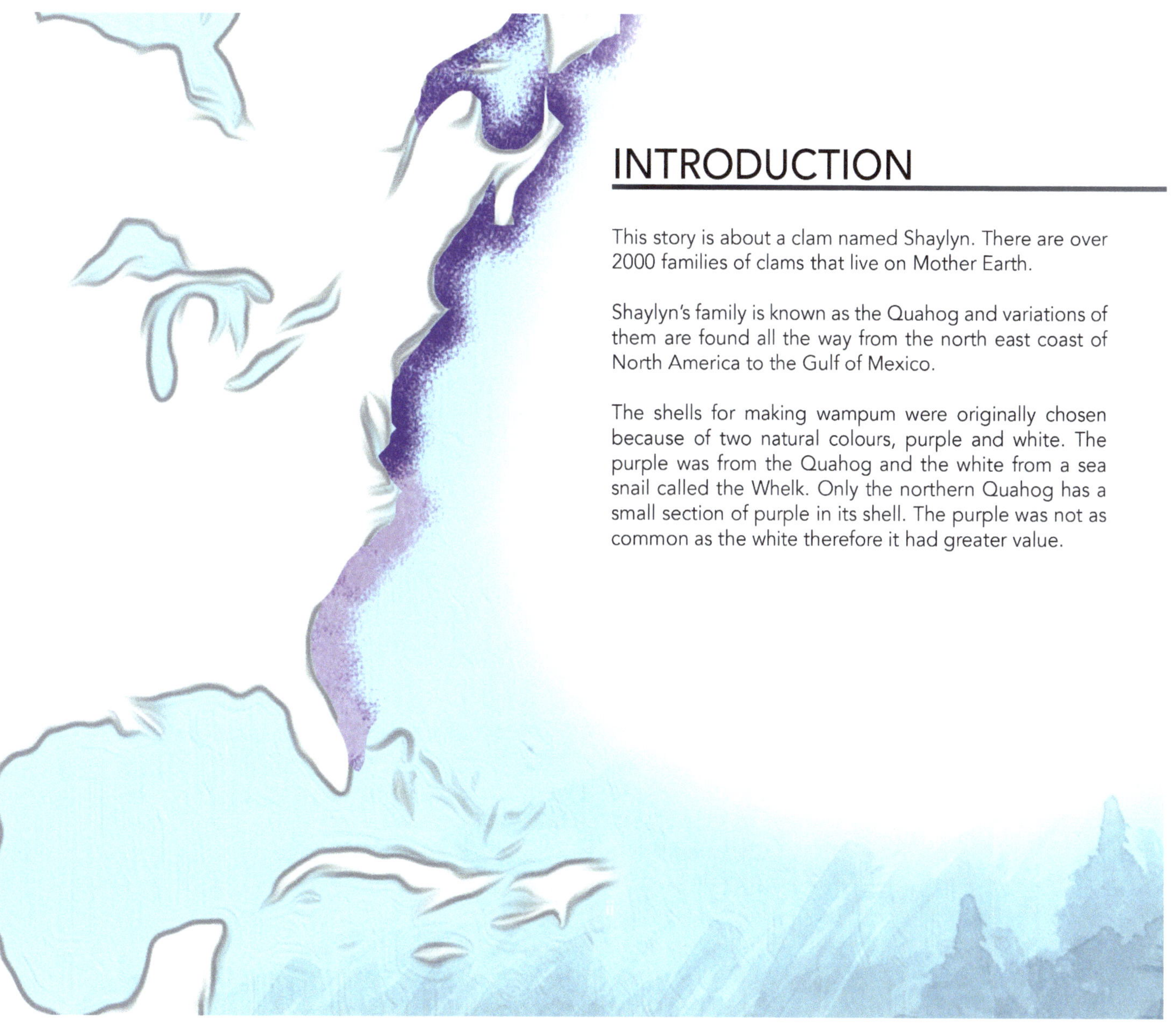

INTRODUCTION

This story is about a clam named Shaylyn. There are over 2000 families of clams that live on Mother Earth.

Shaylyn's family is known as the Quahog and variations of them are found all the way from the north east coast of North America to the Gulf of Mexico.

The shells for making wampum were originally chosen because of two natural colours, purple and white. The purple was from the Quahog and the white from a sea snail called the Whelk. Only the northern Quahog has a small section of purple in its shell. The purple was not as common as the white therefore it had greater value.

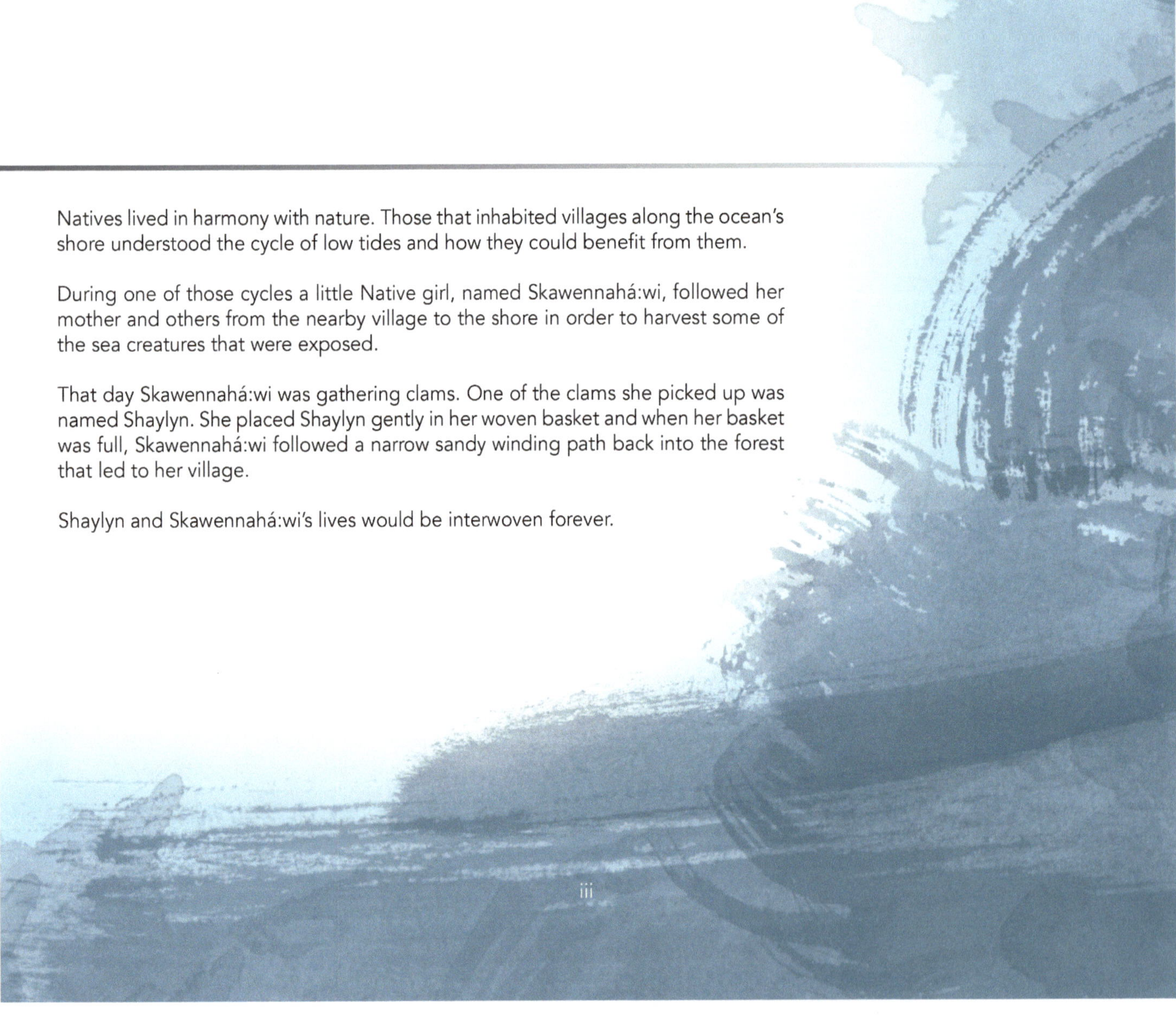

III

Natives lived in harmony with nature. Those that inhabited villages along the ocean's shore understood the cycle of low tides and how they could benefit from them.

During one of those cycles a little Native girl, named Skawennahá:wi, followed her mother and others from the nearby village to the shore in order to harvest some of the sea creatures that were exposed.

That day Skawennahá:wi was gathering clams. One of the clams she picked up was named Shaylyn. She placed Shaylyn gently in her woven basket and when her basket was full, Skawennahá:wi followed a narrow sandy winding path back into the forest that led to her village.

Shaylyn and Skawennahá:wi's lives would be interwoven forever.

Grandmother Moon and Elder Brother Sun pull the water away from the Ocean's shore every day. During this period of low tide, sea creatures are exposed above the water and become easy prey to other animals and humans that want to catch them.

Everything that lives on earth depends on the sun's energy, the air, the water, and on other living things for nourishment and for food. The cycle of life has a beginning and an end. This was known and accepted by all of life's creatures.

Shaylyn, a Quahog clam, lived close to the seashore with many of her clam relatives. She lived underwater and spent most of her time hidden beneath the sand. When feeding, Shaylyn filtered tiny sea creatures, such as plankton, through her shell.

Skawennahá:wi, a young Native girl, had a beautiful spirit. She walked comfortably alone on a quiet part of the beach. Each time Skawennahá:wi picked up a clam she paused before placing it into her basket. It was as if she was greeting each one.

In the past Shaylyn had watched as other clams were gathered by humans and taken away. What happened to them was a mystery. Today, among others, it was Shaylyn who was picked up by Skawennahá:wi. 'Where will I be taken?', Shaylyn wondered.

Skawennahá:wi carried her basket of clams to the village and gently emptied it near a fire pit. The women sitting there began to open the clams, placing the contents into a pot of boiling water. They were making food for the village; clam chowder!

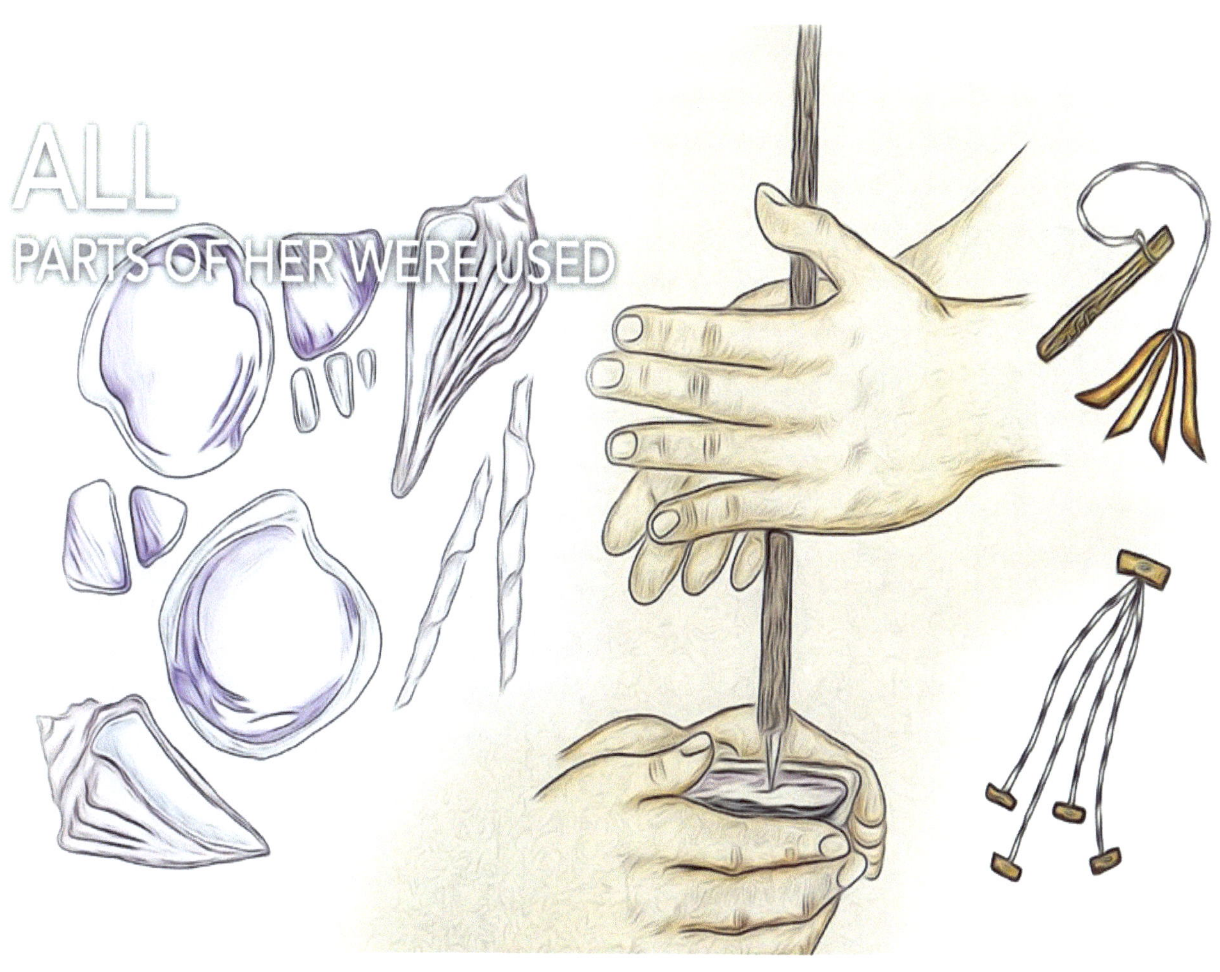

Shaylyn's shell was carefully broken into pieces. The purple sections were collected and chipped into smaller thicker pieces through which holes were drilled. They were then rolled and sanded on a rock until they were tubular in shape and all the same length.

Clamshells were used as cups for drinking water, tools for scraping and cleaning animal hides as well as scoops for grains that were kept in baskets. They were also bound to short or long wooden handles making hoes to be used in small gardens and large fields.

A caterpillar is born from an egg that is laid by a butterfly. The caterpillar spends the next several weeks eating and becoming strong. In just a few short weeks the caterpillar makes a chrysalis. Inside the chrysalis one of nature's many miracles takes place.

Mother Nature always knows when the time is right. What was once a hungry squiggly caterpillar, is allowed to slowly wriggle out of its chrysalis as a beautiful multi-coloured butterfly. It did not die but only changed form. The cycle of life starts all over again.

Just like the butterfly, Shaylyn, the little clam, was changed into something different. The pieces of her shell were shaped into wampum. What she once was, she is no longer. Shaylyn now has a different purpose and a new meaning. She still lives.

Wampum was, and still is, used to make important strings and belts. Each carried, and continue to carry, words spoken into them. These words hold the spiritual essence of the people, their history and their agreements. The wampum belts are a living record.

This is a story of Hayenwah:tha and the first use of condolence strings and the evolution of wampum. Hayenwah:tha had endured great suffering at the hands of an evil sorcerer who was responsible for the death of seven of his daughters. This became unbearable so he wandered into the wilderness.

After many days of walking Hayenwah:tha became quite exhausted and found a place to rest. The next morning, his grief again overwhelmed him. Struggling on, he entered a small clearing where many sumac bushes grew, and there he decided to sit down for a while. As he mourned his seven daughters, he began to cut sumac twigs into small pieces and string them together. As he made the strings of sumac (or elderberry), he said "I will attach words of sympathy to each string, and those words will comfort others who are suffering as I am."

Hayenwah:tha carefully packed the strings in his pouch and continued his journey until he found a small lake where thousands of ducks were feeding. Saying out loud, "Lift up the water and allow me to cross", he watched in awe as this enormous flock of ducks rose, the force of their wings and lifted the water with them. Humbled by what had happened, Hayenwah:tha made his way across the dry bed of the lake. As he walked, he noticed a large number of clam shells laying everywhere. He knew there was a special reason for the shells, so he gathered some and put them in his pouch.

For many hours he travelled south. Later that afternoon he found a clearing and once again sat down. He took the clam shells out of his pouch and began to string them together much like he did with the sumac twigs. Hayenwah:tha then placed two poles into the ground joining them with a smaller branch on top. On the vertical branch he hung each of the strings of sumac along with the shell strings. As he started to speak his words of condolence, a tall man from the Oneida Nation watched him from a distance. The man ran to his village and reported to his Chief what he had seen. An invitation was extended to Hayenwah:tha to come to the village, which he accepted.

After many long days of travel, the Peacemaker arrived at the edge of the Oneida village. He lit a fire and waited for the people to acknowledge his presence. Oneida warriors greeted him and escorted him into the village compound. Following the tradition of hospitality, feast and rest, the Peacemaker was taken to the lodge of Hayenwah:tha. The two men spoke at great length, and then the Peacemaker touched Hayenwah:tha, telling him he would console him and help remove the grief and anger from his heart. He asked Hayenwah:tha to bring out his condolence strings and the clam shells he kept in his deerskin pouch. The Peacemaker created six more strings of wampum made from the shells.

In a ceremony of condolence, the Peacemaker addressed Hayenwah:tha with many words of wisdom and kindness. He handed him a condolence string which became the very first use of wampum in this manner. The Peacemaker then repeated the consoling words several times, and each time he gave Hayenwah:tha a condolence string, until finally, Hayenwah:tha was made clear in mind, spirit and body.

War Belt
Unity of Clans Belt
Ever Growing Tree Belt
William Penn Belt

Fort Stanwix Treaty Belt
French Mission Belt
This is an artistic display of seven wampum belts. The Wampum Shop website explains their meaning.
Champlain Record Belt

A woman making a wampum belt using one of many techniques.

18

DEFINITIONS & ACKNOWLEDGEMENTS

BASKETS were made for transportation, food storage and food preparation. A variety of plant materials were used for weaving baskets; black ash, sweet grass and cornhusks.

CHRYSALISES are made by caterpillars out of which come butterflies. Cocoons are made by moths.

CLAM CHOWDER was made by mixing and cooking the meat from clams and fish with vegetables and spices.

ELDER BROTHER SUN The Haudenosaunee people refer to the animals as brothers and sisters, the earth as Mother, the Moon as Grandmother. All things are related.

FIVE NATIONS were originally the Mohawk, Onondaga, Oneida, Cayuga and Seneca. The Tuscarora were invited into the league early in the 18th century.

GRANDMOTHER MOON: In the Haudenosaunee Creation Story Skywoman fell from sky world to earth and gave birth to a girl. Skywoman later died and became the moon.

HAOHYOH, aka Ken Maracle, is a Lower Cayuga Longhouse Faith Keeper, Deer clan from the Grand River Six Nations. Haohyoh made the wampum belts depicted in the photos throughout the book. His web, The Wampum Shop, has more examples of wampum belts with explanations.

HAYENWAH:THA was invited by the Peacemaker to play a key role contributing to the Great Law of Peace.

LOW TIDE is the pulling of water away from the shore by the gravitational effects of the sun and the moon. When they are aligned with the earth, low tide is most obvious. High Tide is when the pull is toward the shore.

MINUTILLO, ANNETTE retired Executor Director of Braemar House School in Brantford Ontario. She is a friend as well as a valued contributor to my publications.

PLANKTON (singular is Plankter) are made up of a variety of tiny organisms that float in bodies of water and are a very important source of food for many sea creatures.

QUAHOG AND WHELK are both found on the eastern shore of North America from the mouth of the St. Lawrence River to the Gulf of Mexico. The purple part of the Quahog is hard and requires more effort to form into wampum while the white conical and softer Whelk was easier to shape.

SHAYLYN is a real person, my daughter. At the time of her birth her name was not found in a 'book of names' but was actually created as a composite of two names, her mother's and a little girl from the Caribbean. Her good traits are love, adventure, excitement and freedom.

SIX NATIONS IROQUOIS PROG. TEACHERS RES. GUIDE (pgs. 23-25) is the source of the story of Hayenwah:tha found on pages 13-14. The story was written by Raymond R. Skye.

SKAWENNAHÁ:WI in the Mohawk language means; "she is bringing a word/voice/language again,". The name and translation was provided by Sakoiatentha aka Darren Bonaparte, Akwesasne Territory and Karhowane aka Cory McCumber, Kahnawake Territory.

SUMAC was used by Hayenwah:tha to make the first known wampum strings. Sumac grows as a bush or a small tree and is recognized by its red or white flowers.

WAMPUM (singular or plural) were made from natural shells, Quahog and Whelk. Wampum was worn and traded but care should be taken when referring to wampum as 'money'. Wampum was strung into wampum belts and strings, each serving a specific purpose.

WAMPUM belts came in many sizes and before contact with Europeans were made of natural shells. Some belts were known to have over 10,000 wampum in them. After contact they were artificially manufactured in Europe.

WAMPUM STRINGS were, and are, made from the shells of the Quahog and the Whelk. They come as single strings or in particular groupings. The Indigenous Knowledge Centre at Six Nations Polytechnic has more detailed information.

WOODLAND CULTURAL CENTRE, located on the Grand River Six Nations Territory, provided the Two Row Belt as seen on the back cover, courtesy of Paula Whitlow, curator.

WOMAN MAKING A WAMPUM BELT (pg.17) Manuela Torto, model, mentor and family friend.

20

Zig Misiak : is a highly respected, multi award-winning Canadian author of First Nations books and educational resources. As a child, often on his own, Zig became very curious about the children "across the bridge" at the nearby residential (mush-hole) school in Brantford, Ontario. Then, as an adult, he embraced and cultivated interest and enduring relationships with his neighbours and friends, the Haudenosaunee, the Grand River Six Nations People.

Queen Elizabeth II Diamond Jubilee Medal
Sovereign's Medal
Lieutenant Governor's Ontario Heritage Award for Lifetime Achievement
Polish Army Gold Medal - 1st Degree
Canadian Polish Congress Award of Merit
Polish Combatants' Bronze Cross
Shining Star Award
George and Olive Seibel Award
Inductee: Ancaster High School Hall of Distinction
Canadian Aboriginal Veterans Association Medallion

Zig Misiak, became a well-known historical re-enactor who has travelled thousands of miles across Eastern Canada and the United States, participating in the re-enacting of major historical events from the French and Indian Wars, American Revolution, to the War of 1812. He also served in the Canadian Army, Royal Hamilton Light Infantry.

He is now recognized as an authority and a legend for his knowledge, understanding, and commitment to authenticity, as well as the strong friendships he has developed. He has studied and travelled to the very places he has written about in his many books. Zig has a deep love and respect for Indigenous People, recognizing that in spite of the many difficult challenges they have faced, they have remained true to their treaties. As Zig says, **"We must know them."**

Jennifer Bettio, born and raised in Guelph Ontario, is an arts and photography graduate of Sheridan College. With support of her parents she pursued her interests in the arts field that has brought her great success. She does commissioned paintings, art, graphics and design, advertising, illustrations and unique photography. Her French Canadian Métis background, allows her to exhibit a unique First Nations and Métis style of art.